SEVEN AMAZING AFRICAN QUEENS AND DYNASTIES

PUSCH COMMEY

REAL AFRICAN WRITERS (RAW) SERIES

FICTION

Sea Never Dry – ages 4 to 7
Tofi and the Rainbow Fish – ages 7 to 11
Tofi's Fire Dance – ages 12+
Between Sindi and the Sea – ages 12+

NON-FICTION

Great Queens and Kings of Africa – ages 4 to 7
The Glory of African Kings and Queens – ages 7 to 11
Great African Scientists – ages 12+ (forthcoming)
Great African Women – ages 12+ (forthcoming)
Great African Entrepreneurs – ages 12+ (forthcoming)
Great African Leaders of the 20th Century – ages 12+ (forthcoming)

RAW SERIES

Real African stories that inspire, motivate and empower

Facebook: realafricanwriters
www.realafricanwriters.com
www.twitter.com/realafricanwrit

SEVEN AMAZING AFRICAN QUEENS AND DYNASTIES

PUSCH COMMEY

(VOLUME 1)

REAL AFRICAN BOOKS
Powerful African Stories

Real African Books
P. O. Box 145702
Brackengardens
Alberton
1452

0027-82-6928084
Email: Khomasdal69@gmail.com
Facebook Page: Real African Writers

First Published May 2018
Copyright James Pusch Commey
Illustrations: Innocent Dembetembe
Cover Design: Quba
Set in Minion Pro 14pt

Printed and bound in South Africa

All rights reserved. Without limiting the rights under copyright reserved above, no part of this publication may be reproduced, stored in or introduced into a retrieval system or transmitted ,in any form or by any means (electronic, mechanical, photocopying, recording or otherwise) without prior written permission of both the copyright holder and the publisher of the book.

This book is sold subject to the condition that it shall not, by way of trade or otherwise be lent, resold, hired out, or otherwise circulated without the publisher's prior consent in any form of binding or cover other than that in which it is published and without a similar condition being imposed on the subsequent purchaser.

Tribute to a fantastic and awe-inspiring mother – Dorcas Fenimaa Ama Mansa Commey (born Andam). Ex-parliamentarian of the third Republic of Ghana, teacher, celebrated community worker, and a great African Warrior Queen.

14 February 1931 - ?

AUTHOR'S NOTE

For me, it all started as an idle curiosity that led to the book *100 Great African Kings and Queens: Volume One*, with its fantastic illustrations. Its phenomenal success prompted a special dedication: an awe-inspiring chronicle of the exploits of seven African Queens and dynasties. Many thanks to Beulah Mentor-Bux, a fan of *100 Great Kings and Queens*, who suggested the concept for this book. It was a great idea.

While the first book was intended primarily for young people, *Seven Amazing African Queens and Dynasties*, which is also an easy read, was written for both young and old with references for further reading. It includes revised versions of some of the queens in the first book with the addition of stories of a new selection of queens and dynasties. The sheer volume of untold African history means there must be even more amazing African queens who are yet to be discovered.

I was lucky to have come into contact with one of the best book illustrators in the business, Innocent Dembetembe. Without his wonderful illustrations, the stories would not have come alive.

Ultimately it is my hope that these books will inspire more curiosity about Africa's history untold and foster a need in our children to take an interest in their history and retrace their powerful past.

Pusch Komiete Commey

TABLE OF CONTENTS

1. The Rain Queens of Southern Africa 8

2. Yaa Asantewaa – Ashanti Warrior Queen 19

3. Nzinga Of Matamba 28

4. Amina Of Zazzua...35

5. Cleopatra VII: The Last Pharaoh of Egypt 40

6. The Kandakes of Nubia 48

7. Makeda – Queen Of Sheba...59

THE RAIN QUEENS OF SOUTHERN AFRICA

Send down the rain

In the Limpopo province of South Africa you will find the 530-hectare Modjadji Cycad Reserve, the largest concentration of a single cycad species in the world. Some cycads are as old as 280 million years and were once the main diet of prehistoric mammal-like reptiles that lived there.

In the reserve, the Modjadji cycad (*Encephalaros transvenosus*) forms a unique natural forest that can be seen in its natural prehistoric state, thanks to African cultural practices and successive generations of the Modjadji dynasty, who are popularly known as the Rain Queens of southern Africa. The Rain Queens are the hereditary rulers of the area and are celebrated as some of the greatest conservationists of all time. Their rich history dates back more than 400 years.

Recognized as a world heritage site by Unesco, the Modjadji Cycad Reserve is home to part of a genus of 29 species. These plants are a thousand years old and bear cones that weigh up to 34 kilograms. The reserve is also home to the largest baobab tree in the world. It is 22 metres tall with a circumference of 47 metres. Thousands of tourists visit the reserve every year.

The land of the Modjadji is one of few African matriarchal societies. It is situated in the Balobedu district of Lebowa, north-east of the town Duiwelskloof (Devil's gorge), in South Africa. The area contains some of the most fascinating plant species in the world.

There are Balobedu villages on the outskirts of the reserve, where you can experience traditional architecture, language, crafts and culture. Only women may enter the Modjadji village.

WHO ARE THE RAIN QUEENS?

The Rain Queens inspired the well-known work of fiction, *She, A History of Adventure,* by the British writer Sir Henry Rider Haggard (1856–1925). Haggard served as a colonial administrator in the British Natal province of South Africa. He was fascinated with the traditions of the Rain Queens. His record of their narratives and characters is still in print and is said to have sold over 100 million copies to date and still selling today. In movies, the Rain Queen was depicted as a mysterious white woman called Ayesha – she who must be obeyed.

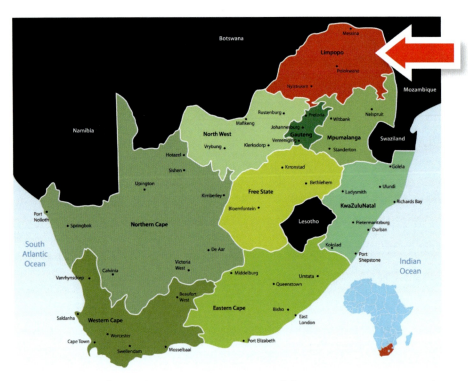

Map of South Africa. The Limpopo Province of the Rain Queens (Top right)

The Modjadjis have produced six rain queens whose history and lineage can be traced back to the Mapungubwe Kingdom and civilization (1075–1220 AD). Mapungubwe later morphed into the illustrious Munhumutapa (Hills of the Jackals) empire, which was also known as Monomatapa by the Portuguese who traded in that area between 1430 and 1760. The empire spanned present-day Zimbabwe, and parts of Zambia, Mozambique, South Africa and Botswana.

Archaeologists have found many golden artefacts at the site of the historical territory of Mapungubwe in South Africa, the most famous of which are a small golden model of a rhinoceros and a golden sceptre.

The empire's gold mines date from 8 AD. It is estimated that they produced about 700 tons of pure gold a year. Sir Rider Haggard captured the stupendous wealth of these mines in another famous novel, *King Solomon's Mines*. The wealth of the biblical King Solomon was believed by some Europeans to be located in the Munhumutapa Empire, which they called Ophir.

THE STORY OF THE MODJADJI

There are many stories of the Rain Queens but the best-known is that of an old chief of the great Munhumutapa who, during a dry spell, was commanded by the ancestors to impregnate Dzugundini, the daughter of King Munhumutapa. They said that if he did so she would gain rain-making skills and end the famine.

Another story says that for the same reason the chief's son impregnated Dzungundini – an abomination that forced her to flee the village. Dzungundini went to the Molotsotsi Valley, in the present-day Balobedu Kingdom. The village she established was later ruled by male leaders, until its matrilineage was re-established.

Oral tradition states that Dzungundini's mother stole several rainmaking charms, namely ostrich feathers, other red and blue beads and a piece of an assegai (spear), to help her fleeing daughters and followers to prosper. The fugitives settled in a mountainous area that is now known as Modjadjiskloof, the location of the Modjadji Cycad Reserve.

A cycad plant in bloom. Although the surrounding district is relatively dry, a mist-belt has resulted in the only pure cycad tree forest in southern Africa. Nearby is the Rain Queen's kraal (homestead).

Dzugundini's son, Makalipe, was born around 1600. He would be the first of six male rulers of the Balobedu over the next two centuries. The story goes that it was during the reign of the fifth king, Keale, that the seed of the matrilineal royal family was restored. Keale, a polygamist, was angered when some of his older sons showed inappropriate interest in his younger spouses. He decreed that succession would not automatically go to the oldest son, but instead through the teachings and approval of the ancestors.

Keale taught his youngest son Mokoto the Balobedu rainmaking rituals. When Keale died, the traditional Balobedu hut-opening ceremony was held. A hut situated in the royal kraal had to be opened. Any person, male or female, who was able to open the hut would be the royal successor, according to the high priest of the ancestors. The will of the ancestors is never questioned.

The story goes that Mokoto, who was a boy at the time, was not universally accepted as the sixth king. When his own sons later threatened to kill one another, he secretly trained his daughter, Modjadji, in the rainmaking rituals. After he died, in 1800, it was Modjadji who opened the hut.

"This one is the chosen one," said the high priest. Modjadji thus succeeded her father and continued the matrilineal leadership heritage until today.

GENERATIONS OF MODJADJIS

Modjadji I ruled for 54 years and was succeeded by her only daughter, Masalanabo. But Masalanabo, who ruled from 1854 to 1894, was childless, which created a succession problem.

However, the Rain Queen traditionally takes "wives", in effect, ladies-in-waiting, from four royal families. Her "bride" from the Makhubo family bore a son and a daughter. This girl, Khesetoane, acceded to the throne in 1895.

Khesetoane's daughter, Makoma, became the fourth Rain Queen in 1959. When Makoma's only daughter, Mokope, became Rain Queen in 1981, she designated her second daughter, Makheala, as her successor.

But Makheala died in 2001, two days before Mokope herself passed away. Makheala's daughter, Makobo, thus became the sixth (and youngest) Rain Queen. She took the throne in 2003. Light rain on the day of her coronation was regarded as a good omen, but two years later she fell ill and died at the age of 27. Her daughter, Masalanabo, who was only three months old when her mother died, will become the seventh rain queen.

In the interim, Masalanabo's uncle, Prince Mpapatla, acts as the Balobedu regent – the first man to rule over his people, albeit in a caretaker capacity, in over 200 years. Rainmaking duties are handled by the women in the royal family.

The documented list of rain queens is as follows:
- Maselekwane Modjadji I (1800–1854)
- Masalanabo Modjadji II (1854–1894)

- Khesetoane Modjadji III (1895–1959)
- Makhoma Modjadji IV (1859–1980)
- Mokope Modjadji V (1981–2001)
- Makobo Modjadji VI (2003–2005)

THE MAGIC OF THE RAIN QUEENS

The Balobedu's precious rainmaking charms are kept under lock and key until the first Saturday in October, when the Balobedu nation gathers at the royal *kraal* in the Balobedu district. Shoes are strictly forbidden in the *kraal*.

A cow named Makhubo is led into the *kraal*. Beer is poured and praises are sung. The traditionally brewed beer is offered to the cow. When the cow has had enough, it is led out of the *kraal* with the other cattle.

The remaining beer is taken to a special shrine adjacent to the *kraal*, where the rainmaking charms are laid out. Skins are laid out around the shrine. The elders sit to one side. While the people praise the queen, the beer is poured over the charms as the Rain Queen calls on the ancestors to make rain.

The medicine to induce the rain is stored in a pot called the *mehago*. When the medicine is burned in a magical horn, the smoke rises into the sky and seeds the rain clouds. The magical horn is placed on the ground while rain continues to fall. When the Rain Queen wishes the rains to stop she hangs up the horn.

After a complex traditional beer-drinking ritual is completed by those present, the big drums are produced and songs for unity are sung, while the people dance around the shrine. Then the ceremony returns to the *kraal* where the nation dances for the rest of the day. Children also take smaller drums and run around the village singing.

Makhubo, the cow used in the rainmaking ceremony, also has a matrilineal heritage. When she gives birth to a female calf, that calf then takes the Makhubo name, just as successive rain queens take the name of Modjadji, the first queen.

THE RADIANCE OF THE QUEEN

Modjaji I became so powerful that even the militaristic Zulus who cut a swathe through South Africa in the 19th century feared them and would not dare set foot in her territory. They gave her the name Mabelemane (four breasts) and believed the fertility and richness she brought to the earth was mirrored by her body. The Zulu King, Shaka, is said to have asked for the blessings of Modjadji I.

Masalanabo Modjadji VII, who must be obeyed, was born in 2005 and is the earthly representative of the rain goddess. Her mother Modjadji VI was the first Rain Queen to be formally educated. Masalanabo has followed in her mother's footsteps by pursuing a global education together with her traditional one.

After a long campaign, the rain queens have been officially recognized under South African law and the royal palace remains at Modjadjiskloof. The South African government declared its recognition of the Balobedu queenship in 2016.

The queenship was discontinued by the apartheid government in 1972. On 9 April, 2018, the President of the Republic of South Africa, Cyril Ramaphosa, officially recognized the queenship and the Rain Queen elect, at a grand coronation ceremony at the Mokwakwaila Stadium outside Modjadjiskloof in the Limpopo province. Masalanabo will officially be installed as the 7th Rain Queen after she has graduated through the Lobedu (Balobedu) customs, and when she turns 18.

There was rainfall on the day of the ceremony following a rainmaking song and dance, which prompted the Rain Queen elect to declare a confirmation of a new dawn for her people.

Masalanabo is regarded by her community as a sacred person and represents a spiritual sense of identity and special powers, just as Catholic people think of the pope. After she is crowned, Masalanabo will marry several maiden women and pay their families *lobola* – the bride price traditionally paid by a husband to his wife's family.

The wives' children with other royal relatives are counted as the queen's own. She too can have children but only with a relative whose identity remains secret. South Africa's constitution legalized same-sex marriage in 2006. Some countries in the world have done the same in the 20th and 21st centuries, but the amazing rain queens have been doing that for hundreds of years.

Yaa Asantewaa
Ashanti Warrior Queen

If you the men of Ashanti
will not go forward
Then we will
We the women will

Between 1824 and 1901, the British Empire fought a series of wars against the Ashanti Empire, which was located in present-day Ghana. It was a determined effort to crush the Ashanti, colonize them and make them part of the British Gold Coast. The Ashanti warrior nation was then among the wealthiest and strongest powers in West Africa and would not allow the British to govern them. This famous series of conflicts is known as the Anglo-Ashanti Wars.

After a number of earlier encounters, the first Anglo-Ashanti war broke out on 21 January, 1824. The British Governor, Sir Charles MacCarthy led an invading force from the coastal town, Cape Coast, into the interior and confronted the Ashanti Army in the battle of Nsamankow. It did not go well for the British, who were completely overrun. The governor was shot dead and beheaded. Almost all the British troops and their local allies, the Fante, numbering over 3 000 troops, were killed.

The Ashanti region in Ghana

The second war was fought in August 1826. The new British governor of the Gold Coast, John Hope Smith, organized a new army in alliance with the Denkyira, local enemies of the Ashanti. New weaponry – Congreve Rockets – were wheeled to Accra, another coastal town. The Ashanti swept down in their numbers from the interior to the coast to attack Accra. The fierce battle that ensued ended in a stalemate, when the Ashanti army was forced back by the shock of the explosions, rocket trails and flying shrapnel. In 1831, a treaty was signed recognizing the Pra River as the border that confined the Ashanti to the interior of present day Ghana. This led to a 30-year peace.

Hostilities resumed when a third war erupted, between 1873 and 1874, when the British decided to take over the gold-rich kingdom. General Garnet Wolseley marshalled 2 500 troops and thousands of West Indian and African troops on a military expedition against the Ashanti.

Elaborate plans were made. Specialized forces and engineers were sent to beat a path through the dense forest to Kumasi, the Ashanti capital. The battle of Amoaful ended in the defeat of the Ashanti when the British entered Kumasi, destroyed parts of it and demolished the royal palace. The British were said to have been impressed by the size of the palace and the rows of books in many languages that they found. The treaty of Fomena was signed with harsh conditions, and the war ended. The King of the Ashanti, Kofi Karikari, was ordered to pay 50 000 ounces of gold as war indemnities. This imposition created a cause for further conflict.

The fourth war is also known as the Second Ashanti Expedition after the previous success of General Wolseley. It lasted only briefly, from December 1895 to February 1896. The British, who were facing competition from French and German forces, offered to make the Ashanti Empire a protectorate in 1891. King Agyeman Prempeh I refused to surrender his sovereignty. Despite an offer of concessions by the king, the British had already made up their mind to annex the empire and its riches. A massive, heavily armed expeditionary force of British and West Indian troops descended on Kumasi with Maxim guns and 75mm artillery.

Major Baden Powell had already paved the way through the thick forest by organizing teams of several local tribes to build bridges, drain marshes, set up camps and tame the forest. The ideas he gathered from the tribes later formed the basis of the global Boy Scout movement, when he published his book *Scouting for Boys* in 1908. From the Ashanti he also learnt the phrase "Slowly, slowly, catch a monkey".

Soon the British Governor, William Maxwell, arrived in Kumasi and demanded the payment of 50 000 ounces of gold indemnities. Unable – or unwilling – to pay, King Prempeh was deposed, arrested and forced to sign a treaty of protection. He and other Ashanti leaders were sent into exile in the Seychelles.

THE FIFTH WAR AND THE RISE OF YAA ASANTEWAA

The fifth war, in 1900, became known as the War of the Golden Stool. It gave rise to the legend of Yaa Asantewaa, the Queen mother of Ejisu.

This time, the British had taken over the gold mines of the Ashanti and made them pay heavy taxes. The fiercely independent Ashanti were very unhappy. They had no income to govern themselves. Those who disagreed were thrown into jail. As part of the colonization process, British missionary schools were established to impose their religion on the Ashanti and mentally drill them to accept their rule. When the missionaries started to interfere in local affairs, the Ashanti seethed with anger. But worse was to come.

The Ashanti have a sacred stool made of pure gold that embodies the soul of the kingdom. According to Ashanti history, in the 17th century, when the kingdom took shape, it was commanded from the sky during a great festival by the High Priest, Okomfo Anokye. Nobody is permitted to sit on the stool, not even the kings, who derive their authority from it. Only royals may see it. Replicas are displayed in public during important festivals when the king makes an appearance and people gather to celebrate the renewal of the kingdom.

One day, the British Governor, Lord Frederick Mitchell Hodgson, demanded that the Ashanti surrender the golden stool for him to sit on. His insistence was extremely arrogant, and provocative. "How could he sit on our soul?" they whispered in shock and disbelief. It was a cause worth dying for.

A certain Captain Armitage was instructed to round up the Ashanti and force them to reveal the whereabouts of the golden stool. After going from village to village without success, Armitage learnt through his spies that the village of Bare had custody of the stool. He surrounded the village but found only children at play. On interrogating the children with his interpreters, he was told that the parents had gone hunting. He accused them of lying and ordered them to be flogged until they revealed the whereabouts of their parents.

When the parents heard the wailing of their children they came out of hiding to defend them. They too were bound and severely beaten. Armitage then rounded up the chiefs and ordered them to produce the golden stool or face serious consequences. They were thrown into jail when they denied knowledge of the whereabouts of the stool.

In the absence of their king, the remaining chiefs were afraid to go up against the might of the British Empire. A secret meeting of the surviving members of the Ashanti government met to discuss the return of their king. There was a lot of disagreement on how to go about solving the British problem. It was then that Yaa Asantewaa rose up and addressed the council with these famous words:

> *Now I see that some of you fear to go forward to fight for your King. If it were the brave days of Osei Tutu, Okomfo Anokye and Opoku Ware, chiefs will not sit down and see their king taken away without firing a shot. No European would have dared speak to the Chiefs of Asante in the way the governor speaks to you. Is it true that the bravery of Asante is no more? I cannot believe it. It cannot be! I must say this: If you the men of*

Asante will not go forward, then we will. We the women will. I shall call upon my fellow women. We will fight. We will fight until the last of us falls in the battlefields.

The speech shocked the men into action. They were so ashamed of themselves that they decided to pick up arms and fight. They chanted, "If I go forward I die, If I go backwards, I die. Better to go forward."

THE SIEGE OF THE KUMASI FORT

On March 28, 1900, Yaa Asantewaa mobilized the Ashanti troops and laid siege to the British mission at the Fort of Kumasi. The British had to bring in several thousand troops and heavy artillery to break the siege. In retaliation, British troops plundered villages, killed most of the people, confiscated their lands and left the remaining population dependent on the British for survival. Superior technology and weaponry made all the difference in the 100-year battle to subjugate the Ashanti Kingdom, which neither courage, determination nor fighting skills did. The battle cry of the Ashanti until today is "If you kill a thousand, a thousand more will come forward."

Yaa Asantewaa was captured during the siege, as she fired her guns. She and other leaders, were exiled to the Seychelles, while most of the other chiefs became prisoners of war.

The kingdom was forced to become a British protectorate. On 1 January, 1902, the Ashanti territories became part of the British Gold Coast colony on condition that the golden stool remained sacred and was not violated. To the Ashanti, the defence of the stool was a monumental victory. The well-hidden stool, which appears on the Ashanti flag, was discovered by accident by road workers much later in 1920. Until today it remains very much a proud symbol of the Ashanti.

Eventually, the exiled King Prempeh and his chiefs were allowed to return home on December 27, 1924 with the remains of Yaa Asantewaa who had died in exile on October 17, 1921. She was given a burial fit for a heroine.

The Kwame Nkrumah Mausoleum and memorial park in downtown Accra, the capital of Ghana

A few decades later, in 1957, the Ashanti Kingdom, as part of the Gold Coast, fought for and gained independence under the illustrious leadership of its first Prime Minister, Dr Kwame Nkrumah. The Gold Coast was renamed Ghana after the ancient powerful and wealthy Ghana Empire, which flourished in West Africa from 300 AD to 1100 AD.

Yaa Asantewaa remains a very popular folk heroine in the history of Ghana and an inspiration to many Ghanaians and Africans.

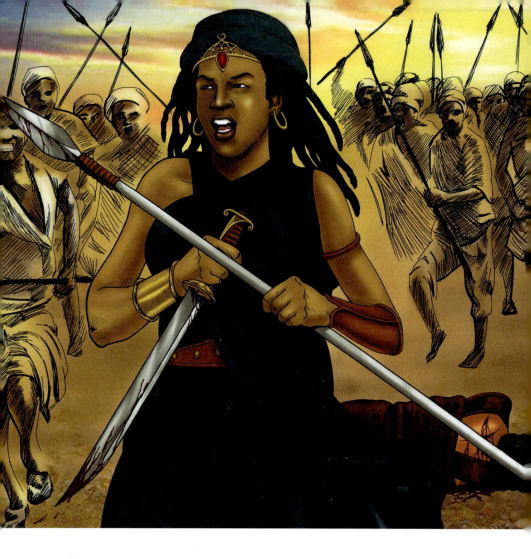

NZINGA OF MATAMBA

You must call me king

Nzinga, Queen of Matamba is known as one of the most formidable freedom fighters of all time. She was born to Njinga a Mbande Ngola Kiluaje and Guenguela Cakombe around 1582 in the kingdom of Matamba, in the country known today as Angola. She was named Njinga according to tradition, because when she was born her umbilical cord was wrapped around her neck. In the language she spoke, Kimbundu, *kujinga* means to twist or turn.

Nzinga was a great military leader. She fought hard to resist the Portuguese of those days who raided her kingdom, Ndongo, in search of slaves and economic gain. She always led from the front.

Nzinga was also a skilled diplomat and peacemaker. She made several attempts to make peace with the Portuguese. But when it became clear that the Portuguese were hell-bent on enslaving and plundering her kingdom, she formed a powerful army and fought back. Over a period of 30 years she inflicted heavy defeats on the Portuguese.

According to historical records she was groomed by her father the king who allowed her to sit at his feet as he governed his kingdom. She also accompanied him to war. Nzinga had two sisters – Funji a Mbande and Kambu a Mbande. Her only brother and heir to the throne was Ngola a Mbande.

In 1622, Nzinga accompanied her brother to a peace conference in Luanda with the Portuguese governor, Joao Correia De Sousa. Today, Luanda is the capital of Angola, so named by the Portuguese who thought the name of the king – Ngola – was the name of the territory.

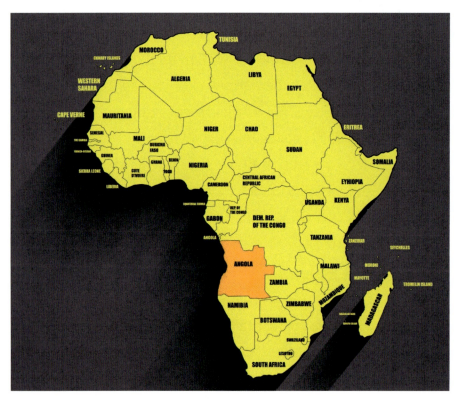

Angola. South West Africa.

Nzinga's brother wanted the Portuguese to remove the slave-holding fortress of Ambaca, built by Governor Luis Mendes De Vasconcelos in 1618. He also insisted on the return of his subjects, called *kijiko*, who had been taken captive to be exported as slaves to Brazil and the West Indies. In their quest for slaves, the Portuguese had also employed local mercenaries called *imbangalas* to help raid villages and capture their own people for sale. Ngola wanted to put a stop to these activities.

A popular story tells of how Governor Correia De Sousa

offered Nzinga no chair to sit on at the beginning of the negotiations and placed a mat on the floor for her while he sat on the governor's chair. In Nzinga's Mbundu custom that was the way subordinates were treated. Nzinga was not willing to accept this and ordered one of her servants to get down on the ground so that she could sit on his back. By doing this she asserted that she was equal to the governor.

Nzinga managed to persuade the governor to accept all her demands. She was so delighted that she converted to Christianity, was baptized and took the name Donna Anna De Sousa, in honour of the governor's wife.

But the treaty was never honoured by the Portuguese who refused to return the *kijikos*, insisting that they were slaves captured in war. Furthermore, they failed to remove the fortress Ambaca and did nothing to stop the *imbangala* from causing havoc.

The loss of control over his kingdom so depressed Nzinga's brother that in 1624 AD he committed suicide. Nzinga assumed control over her people as regent of Kaza, her brother's infant son and heir to the throne. She assumed ruling powers of their kingdom, Ndongo, and called herself Senhora de Dongo (Lady of Ndongo) and later Rainha de Dongo (Queen of Ndongo).

Things came to a head in 1624 when a new Portuguese governor, Fernao de Sousa, arrived and began fresh negotiations with Nzinga. As a starting point he refused to comply with key demands agreed to with his predecessor, Correia de Sousa. He claimed possession of the *kijikos* and refused to shut down Ambaca.

Nzinga declared war on the Portuguese and Fernao de Sousa ousted her from her island capital of Kidonga. She fled to the east but re-occupied the island in 1627. In 1629 she was again driven out and her sister was captured. Portuguese forces and their *imbangala* pursued Nzinga and what remained of her army to the Baixa de Cassange district in the north. Nzinga was cornered but managed to escape by climbing down steep cliffs with ropes.

Unable to hold on to the Kingdom of Ndongo, Nzinga raised sufficient forces to take over the neighbouring Kingdom of Matamba which she accomplished in 1631.

In her campaigns Nzinga personally led her troops into battle and would not allow her subjects to call her queen. She preferred to be addressed as king.

In 1639, Portugal tried to reach an understanding with Nzinga. They sent a mission to Matamba to improve relations but the damage had been done. She could no longer trust them.

GOING DUTCH

In 1641, the Dutch West India Company, rivals of the Portuguese, seized Luanda. Like the Portuguese, the Dutch were also in the slave-trading business, capturing and exporting slaves to the West Indies in the Americas. Their compatriots, the Dutch East

India Company, who sailed around the tip of Africa looking for spices in the East, especially in India, later occupied and colonized the country now known as South Africa.

Nzinga hoped to recover her lost Kingdom of Ndongo with the help of the Dutch and as a result moved her capital to the northern part of Ndongo. In 1644, she formed an alliance with the Dutch, waged war on the Portuguese army and thoroughly defeated them in Ngoleme. Two years later, in 1646, the Portuguese attacked and defeated her at Kavanga. In the process they captured and drowned her other sister Funji in the Kwaanza river.

Again using Dutch supplies of arms and ammunition, Nzinga routed a Portuguese army in 1647 and laid siege on the Portuguese capital, Masangano.

In 1648, the Portuguese recaptured Luanda from the Dutch with the help of a Brazilian commander named Salvador De Sa e Benavides. With the loss of Dutch assistance, Nzinga retreated to Matamba and continued to resist Portugal well into old age.

FINAL YEARS

In 1657, weary from her long struggle, Nzinga eventually signed a peace treaty with Portugal. Most of her demands were accepted by the Portuguese. She devoted her efforts to resettling former slaves and trying to reconstruct her nation, which had been seriously damaged by years of conflict.

Despite many attempts by rivals to dethrone her, Nzinga died a peaceful death at the age of 80 on December 17, 1663. After Nzinga died Matamba went through a protracted civil war, but her legacy lived on. Portugal would no longer have control over the Angolan interior until well into the 20th century when it recolonized the country after the Berlin conference of 1884, organized by Portugal and hosted by the German Chancellor Otto Von Bismark. It became popularly known as the Scramble for Africa. It resulted in the invasion and partition of various African territories amongst European powers. Portugal's gains were reversed in 1975 when Angola re-gained its independence after a protracted war.

Today, the great warrior Nzinga is fondly remembered in Angola. Portugal and much of Europe would come to respect this formidable African queen. In Luanda, a major street is named after her and there is a massive statue of her in Kinaxixi square, a favourite venue for weddings.

As befits a great African icon and towering heroine of Angola, Nzinga is known by many different names, reflecting her fame and popularity. These include Queen Nzinga, Nzinga I, Queen NzingaNdongo, NzingaMbandi, Nzinga Mbande, Jinga, Singa, Zhinga, Ginga, Njinga, Njingha, Ana Nzingha, NgolaNzhinga, Nzinga of Matamba, Zinga, Zingua, Ann Nzingha, Mbande Ana Nzingha, Ann Nzingha, Dona Anna de Sousa, Dona Ana De Souza, Queen Nzinga of Ndongo.

AMINA OF ZAZZUA

Aminatu ta san rana

The great African Queen, Amina Sukhera, ruled the Hausa people of West Africa in the 16th century AD. The Hausa Kingdom was very well organized. Cities were divided into wards and councils with efficient economic and judicial systems. Their economy was built on industry, trade and commerce. It was very well structured and efficient.

Amina (who is also referred to as Aminatu) was a Muslim princess of the royal family of Zazzua in what is now the Zaria province of Nigeria. She was born around 1533 AD and is said to have died in 1610 AD. She is believed to have been the granddaughter of King Zazzua Nohir and was the oldest of three royal children. She later ascended the throne to become the 24th Habe, the title of the rulers of Zazzua.

A popular African proverb says a chick that is destined to grow into a cock can be spotted the very day it hatches. Amina was 16 when her mother, the powerful Bakwa of Turunku, inherited the throne of Zazzua. At an early age Amina began to learn how to rule by taking care of wards and councils in the city. She then trained herself in the Zazzua army.

During the reign of her mother, the teenage Amina occupied herself with acquiring battle skills under the guidance of the Zazzua military command. Zazzua was then in the centre of important trade routes that connected North Africa with south-west and western Sudan.

Her mother was a peaceful Queen who brought great prosperity to the city, but Amina the warrior had other ambitions. On the death of her mother, Amina's brother Karama succeeded to the throne. When Karama died, Amina became the ruler of Zazzua.

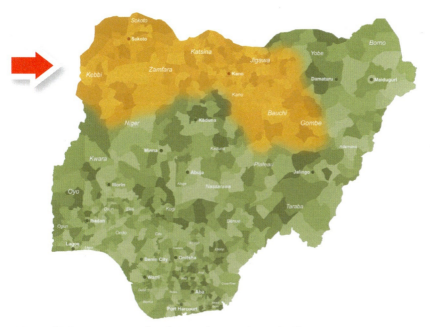

Map of Nigeria. Hausaland is in the northern half.

AMINA'S MILITARY CAMPAIGNS

Within three months of inheriting the throne, Queen Amina embarked on what was to be the first of her military expeditions. She stood in command of an immense military force. She personally led the cavalry of Zazzua, waging battle continuously throughout the course of her 34-year rule. The battle for trade routes between rival states in west Africa caused endless conflicts between the 12th and 17th centuries. Strong leaders were needed to protect their territories.

Rival states like the Jukun and Nupe to the south clashed with Zazzua on several occasions and were defeated. Within this period the Mali, the Fulani and Bornu State also attacked and defeated the Hausa. Military conflicts in that part of west

Africa continued without end. It got worse when the dominant Songhai empire fell in the 16th century, and caused a fight.

At the time, the citizens of Hausaland were very advanced in the industrial arts and science of tanning, weaving and metalwork, while their neighbours in the surrounding areas engaged mainly in agriculture.

The Hausa were also excellent traders. They bought and sold goods such as leather, cloth, kola, salt, horses and metal, but trade was restricted in the areas that were controlled by hostile warlords.

Amina went to war against these warlords to force them to become part of Zazzua and remove obstacles to free trade and safe passage. Hausa State became very prosperous and grew threefold.

Amina conquered all the towns as far as Kwararafa to the north and Nupe to the south. She came to dominate much of the region known as Hausaland and beyond and extended it to incorporate the city states of Rano, Daura, Gobir and Kano.

At one time Amina dominated the entire area, including the associated trade routes that connected Western Sudan with Egypt to the east, and Mali to the north. She collected tributes of kola nuts and male slaves from the conquered cities.

Amina was not all about war and occasionally used diplomacy. Ultimately, she negotiated a ruling arrangement with the Fulani people that brought lasting peace to the region.

GANUWAR AMINA AND HER LEGACY

Amina is perhaps best remembered by what are popularly known as "Ganuwar Amina" or Amina's Walls. Throughout her reign she built walls around the encampments of the territories she conquered. Some of these earth walls have survived and are part and parcel of the culture and landscape of her native Hausa City States.

In the 21st century the memory of Amina has come to represent the spirit and strength of womanhood. For her military exploits she earned the praise name Amina Yar Bakwa ta san rana, which means Amina, daughter of Nikatau, a woman as capable as a man. It is commonly believed that Amina died during a military campaign at Atagara near Bida in modern day Nigeria.

Amina's legacy is immense. Many stories have been told about her, some fact, some fiction, and many a myth. In Hausaland, this has transformed her into a huge inspirational and legendary figure. As testimony to her greatness, a statue stands in her honour at the National Arts Theatre in Lagos, the commercial capital of Nigeria. Many educational institutions in northern Nigeria also carry her name.

CLEOPATRA VII
THE LAST PHARAOH OF EGYPT

I am the Nile

Of all the many ancient great kings and queens of Africa, perhaps the greatest – and least-known –female ruler of Kemet or ancient lower Egypt, was the Pharaoh Hatshesput, also known as Maatkare. She reigned from about 1473 BC to

1458 BC. Not much is known about her because an attempt was made to erase her illustrious legacy, perhaps because she was a woman.

After Hatshesput, the next famous female ruler was Cleopatra VII, who became the last pharaoh of Egypt. Upper Egypt or Nubia, however, had a long line of illustrious female pharaohs known as the Kandakes (referred to in Europe as Candace).

Cleopatra VII Philopator reigned from 51 to 30 BC. She was only seventeen years old when she ascended the throne. She is often said to be of mixed Macedonian and African parentage arising from the Macedonian–Greek conquest, occupation and adoption of the culture and civilization of Kemet – the land of black people. That conquest and occupation started with Alexander the Great, lasted for about 302 years (332 BC–30 BC) and ended with the death of Cleopatra VII through Roman conquest led by Augustus Caesar. She was, however, briefly survived as Pharaoh by her son, Caesarion. After Cleopatra ancient Egypt was reconfigured as a province of the newly established Roman Empire, and would never be the same.

Cleopatra is identified with the Ptolemaic Dynasty (the line of Greek rulers of ancient Egypt, from 305 BC to 30 BC, called the Ptolemies). Her father was King Ptolemy XII, whom she succeeded on his death. Little is known about her mother, who was believed to be of original Kemet or African descent. In life and in death Cleopatra VII was always controversial.

LAST PHARAOH OF EGYPT

Cleopatra was born in 69 BC. She was an intelligent, beautiful, quick-witted, practical and creative woman who was fluent in nine languages. She was also a good mathematician and an excellent businesswoman.

Cleopatra understood the world better than most rulers of her time. She dreamt of becoming the empress of the known world. She might have succeeded if the two men she counted on had not died before her.

She was a born leader who fought tooth-and-nail for her country, with all her heart and soul. In fact, she did everything she could to save Egypt from its chief enemies, the Romans.

The two most powerful rulers of the Romans associated with her were Julius Caesar and Mark Anthony. A third minor co-ruler was Lepidus.

Pharaoh Cleopatra was queen of the spectacular, a show-woman. When Julius Caesar was effective ruler of Rome, it is said that a beautiful Persian carpet was presented to him as a gift from Egypt. When it was unrolled, out tumbled Cleopatra.

Caesar was so charmed by this gesture that he fell for the young Cleopatra. He wooed her and took her as his partner. In due course, Cleopatra gave birth to their child Ptolemy Caesar, in 47 BC. He was named Caesarion, which meant 'little Caesar'.

The goddess Isis – ideal mother and wife.

THE NEW CLEOPATRA-CAESAR ALLIANCE

It was during this time that Julius Caesar abandoned his plans to conquer Egypt and instead helped Cleopatra become the Queen and Pharaoh of Egypt.

But Cleopatra wanted more. She pressured Julius Caesar to name Caesarion heir to the throne of Rome. If Caesarion was heir to both the Roman Empire and Egypt, Cleopatra would be able to unite Africa and Europe. Julius Caesar refused and instead followed tradition and chose his grandnephew Octavian, who later became the Roman emperor, Augustus Caesar.

Julius Caesar loved Cleopatra so much that he planned to marry her against the laws of Rome, which forbade marriage to foreigners. Irrespective of the law, he lived with Cleopatra in his palace and had a gold statue made of them standing side-by-side.

This made the Romans very angry. Their anger boiled over when Cleopatra started calling herself Isis, an ancient goddess of Kemet who was also worshipped by the Romans and Greeks as the ideal wife and mother.

Julius Caesar was murdered in a palace coup in 44 BC and was succeeded by Mark Anthony and Octavian as co-rulers, with a less influential Lepidus. Cleopatra requested a meeting with Mark Anthony. She sailed to meet him in a flotilla of beautifully adorned gondolas, with silver oars and purple sails. She was dressed as Aphrodite, the goddess of love. Stunning Nereid handmaidens steered the oars and her Erotes, a group of winged young godlings, fanned her as the boats sailed.

Like Caesar, Mark Anthony was hit by the thunderbolt of love. He fell head-over-heels in love and worshipped at the feet of Cleopatra. Soon they became lovers. During their relationship, Cleopatra bore twins, a boy and a girl. They were named Alexander Helios and Cleopatra Selene.

Anthony would do anything for Cleopatra. He ordered her name to be put on the face of the Roman coin, the silver Denarius. Then, to the shock of the Romans, he divorced his second wife, Octavia, the sister of his co-ruler Octavian, who was recognized as the first and most influential Roman emperor.

I AM THE NILE

So powerful was Cleopatra that her favourite oath was "As surely as I shall yet dispense justice on the Roman capital."

She then declared: "I am the Nile". The Nile River was the centre of life in the ancient world. The Nile spans the African continent from its source in East Africa until it discharges its waters into the Mediterranean Sea in Egypt. For over 3 000 years the Nile Valley nurtured the greatest civilization known to mankind. Many of the achievements of Ancient Egypt are still a source of wonder and inspiration today.

Octavian declared war on Anthony to avenge the dishonour of his sister's divorce and terminate what he considered the poisonous influence of Cleopatra on the affairs of Rome. Cleopatra sailed with Anthony as a united Egyptian–Roman unit to face off Octavian at the famous battle of Actium. But Octavian prevailed. To avoid capture, Mark Anthony committed suicide, leaving Cleopatra to her fate.

Octavian blamed Cleopatra for the instability she had helped create in Rome. He planned to publicly humiliate her by putting her on display, but Cleopatra was too proud an African to accept such a fate. While in prison she ordered a small but lethal Egyptian cobra (an asp) to be brought to her hidden in a basket of figs, which she put on her arm or breast.

She died on August 12, 69 BC, at the age of 39. The question of how Cleopatra died has been the subject of much controversy. Some say she used a poisonous ointment, while others insist it was a hidden asp brought to her by a rustic (rural man) in a vase of fruit. It is said that she found it after eating some of the fruit and held out her arm for the cobra to bite her. Cleopatra poked and provoked it until it bit her. She was found dead with a maid dying at her feet while another maid adjusted her crown and then also fell. The play *Anthony and Cleopatra*, written many centuries later by the famous English writer, William Shakespeare, gives another version in which Cleopatra dies while clutching the snake to her breast.

Many books, plays, poems and opinion pieces have been written about Cleopatra, testimony to the degree to which she captured the world's imagination during her short life.

Tributes in her honour extolled her as a woman of unsurpassed beauty and state that she was most striking. Some say she possessed a charming voice and was skilled in making herself liked by all and sundry, being brilliant to look upon and listen to, with the power to charm everyone. Others say her beauty was in itself not altogether incomparable, nor such as to strike those who saw her. What ultimately made her attractive was her wit, charm and the sweetness in the tones of her voice.

Cleopatra's last wish was never to be forgotten. She seems to have succeeded. According to Egyptian religious beliefs at the time, death by snakebite would make one immortal.

THE KANDAKES OF NUBIA

Bring us the head of the Roman emperor

The great African civilization of Nubia, in present-day Sudan and part of southern Egypt, originated at the junction of the Atbarah, the Blue Nile and the White Nile rivers. The latter two rivers are the largest tributaries of the most famous river in the world: the River Nile (6 853 km). The civilization that arose in the valley of the Nile, called the land of Black people (Kemet), more than 5 000 years ago, is unrivalled in the history of mankind.

Its sophistication and many astounding inventions still exist in various forms, in, amongst others, the fields of science, mathematics, art, government, religion, philosophy, medicine, architecture, writing and even in the use of speech. The Blue Nile has been linked to the biblical story of creation, in Genesis 2, where it is called the River Gihon, which flowed near the Garden of Eden, located in Uganda.

In the past, the Nile Valley region was known as Upper Egypt and Lower Egypt. Upper Egypt, the higher ground from which the Nile flowed, was mostly Nubia, in Sudan, while

Lower Egypt was for the most part what comprises present-day Egypt.

The name Egypt came about with the Greek conquest and occupation of the lower region from 332 BC to 30 BC (302 years). The Greek translation of Kemet was Aigyptos, or Egypt. In the English-speaking world and other places, the name Egypt has stuck. Arabs invaded North Africa and occupied Egypt from 639 AD with the rise of Islam. Today the Arabs call the country Misr.

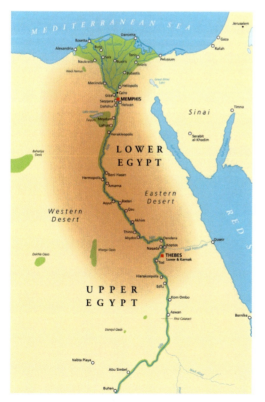

Kemet – land of black people. (Ancient Egypt)

Nubia arose after the collapse of the Bronze Age in 6000 BC. Historians agree that Nubia, also known as Kush or Upper Egypt, was one of the first civilizations to take hold in the Nile Valley along the cataracts of the Nile.

Nubia's first capital was Kerma (2600–1520 BC). In time it was moved to Napata (1000–300 BC) and then further south to the ancient city of Meroë (300 BC–300 AD), with its famous pyramids and writings known as the meroitic script.

THE KANDAKES

Among the long line of famous rulers of Nubia were powerful queens known as the Kandakes. In Europe they were referred to as "Candace". The Nubian kings were called Qore. The first mention of these queens was Kandake Makeda, reputed to have been the Queen of Sheba, in Ethiopia (c.1005 BC to 935 BC). Makeda is said to have paid a famous royal visit to the biblical King Solomon of Judea.

Another famous Nubian Queen was said to be Pelekh, also known as the Kandake of Meroe, who was said to have ruled from 345 BCE to 332 BCE, during which Alexander invaded lower Egypt. Many records state that when Alexander conquered ancient Lower Egypt he tried to push further down south to Nubia (Upper Egypt) but came up against the powerful Kandake, whose massive army entered into formation and marched towards him. Alexander was so frightened that, rather than risk defeat, he beat a hasty retreat.

Although this story is refuted by some historians as legendary, because it comes from an unknown writer in a book called *Alexander Romance*, other historians stand by it.

The tombs of the Kandakes are found in pyramids that cover a large area of the former capital, Meroë. There are about 223 of them as compared to about 138 in present-day Egypt. Hieroglyph writings, the meroitic script, that record their awesome deeds, can be seen in these pyramids. Until today, linguists have struggled to decode the meroitic script, unlike the hieroglyphs of their cousins in Lower Kemet or Egypt which have been translated.

THE CITY OF MEROË

Meroë was a complex, wealthy and advanced society that was politically stable. It relied on elected kingship with elaborate coronation ceremonies in which the queen mother played an important role. Excavations of the large ancient city have revealed huge palaces, royal baths and beautiful temples.

From 300 BC to 300 AD there is a record of some of the best known warrior queens and the period of their reign: Amanirenas (40 BC to 10 BC), Amanishakheto (10 BC to 1 BC) and Amanitore (1BC to 20 AD). Others were Amanikhatashan, Amanitarquine, Amanikhabale, Amantitere, Shanakdkhete, Nawidemak, Lakhideamani, Amanitaraqide and Malequorobar.

AMANIRENAS

Amanirenas is best known as the one-eyed queen who raided the Romans in Lower Egypt and defeated them decisively.

The war lasted five years, from 27 BCE to 22 BCE. Amanirenas has been described as very brave. She was blind in one eye from an injury she received in one of her military campaigns. The raid on the Romans followed the Roman conquest of Lower Egypt (Kemet) by Augustus Caesar (also known as Octavian) in 30 BC, that ended the reign of Cleopatra VII, the last Pharaoh of Egypt.

After the Romans captured Egypt from the Greeks, Augustus Caesar appointed Aellius Gallus as chief magistrate of Egypt. Soon after, in 27 BC, the Nubians began hostilities, which led to a fierce attack in 24 BC. Amanirenas and her son Akinidad annihilated Roman forces along the River Nile at Syene and Philae, and drove the Jews from Elephantine, an island on the River Nile. They returned to Nubia with prisoners and loot, including several statues of Augustus Caesar. Amanirenas then buried a bronze likeness of the emperor beneath the entranceway to her palace so that she and all who came and

went could tread on the head of her enemy. The most complete statue of Augustus ever found was recovered in Meroë. It is housed in the Berlin Museum in Germany.

Meroitic inscriptions give Amanirenas the title of *qore* as well as *kandake* suggesting that she was a ruling queen. The Kushites were driven out of Syene later in the year by another governor – Gaius Petronius – who now held the office of Roman prefect in Egypt. According to a detailed report by the Greek writer Strabo, the Roman troops advanced far into Kush and eventually reached the city of Napata. Although they withdrew again to the north, they left behind a garrison in Qasr Ibrim (Primis), which then became the border of the Roman Empire. The Nubians later launched a series of attacks on Primis.

Exhausted by the onslaughts and mounting pressure, Augustus Caesar was forced to negotiate. In 20 BC, a peace treaty was concluded. It was strikingly favourable to the Nubians, in that the southern part of a contested 80-mile strip including Primis, was evacuated by the Romans. The Romans had in effect capitulated.

The Pyramids of Meroë

So fearsome were the Kandakes that this arrangement continued until the end of 3 AD, with relations between Meroë and Roman Egypt remaining generally peaceful during this time, except for one violation by Augustus Caesar. The Roman emperor once again paid a heavy price against another African Queen, Amanikasheto.

AMANIKASHETO

Amanirenas was succeeded by her daughter Amanikasheto who reigned from 10 BC to 1 AD. Much of what we know about Amani-ka-sheto, also known as Amani-sha-keto, was revealed when the top of her pyramid tomb was blown off with explosives by an Italian grave robber called Giuseppe Ferlini in 1834. It appears that he had no concern for preserving history; Ferlini destroyed 40 pyramids while searching for treasure.

Amanikasheto had been buried with some amazing artefacts – priceless bracelets and rings unrivalled in craftsmanship – which today are housed in the Berlin Museum and in the Egyptian Museum of Munich in Germany. The jewellery includes a golden bracelet with intricate blue engravings, ten bracelets, two armbands, nine shield rings and 67 signet rings.

More information about Amanikasheto is recorded in various monuments in Egypt. There are inscriptions about her in one of her palace buildings, Amen or Amun-temple of Kawa in the ancient Kush town of Wad ban Naqa and stelas at Qasr Ibrim and Naqa (the Arabic names). She was known to be extremely wealthy and held a significant amount of power; she was responsible for the construction of many of the pyramids at Meroë. Her 60-room palace in Wad ban Naqa at 61 metres long and 3 700 square metres in area, is one of the largest ever discovered. Historians believe she practised a religion that was very similar to that of her cousins to the north, in present-day Egypt.

After the peace treaty signed with her mother Amanirenas, Augustus Caesar tried again to push further south to Nubia. He came up against her daughter and heiress Amanikasheto. Again the Roman Empire was thoroughly thrashed, compelling Augustus Caesar to confine himself to Lower Egypt (present-day Egypt) until his dying days.

Both Augustus Caesar (who ruled the Roman empire and its conquered territory of Lower Egypt for 40 years from 27 BC to 14 AD) and the Greek Alexander the Great, were never able to invade and conquer Nubia (Upper Egypt) because of the might of the powerful African Women – the Kandakes.

AMANITORE

Amanitore (1BC–20 AD) succeeded her mother Amanikasheto. In Egyptian hieroglyphics the throne name of Amanitore reads "Merkare". Amanitore is often mentioned as a co-regent of Pharaoh Natakamani. It is uncertain whether she was his mother or his wife. Images of Natakamani frequently include an image of Amanitore.

Texts that mention Amanitore as a ruler include those in the temple at the Nubian capital of Napata, in a temple in Meroë near Shendi and at the Naqa Lion Temple. Her royal palace can be seen at the Unesco heritage site, Gebel Barkal in modern-day Sudan. Amanitore's pyramid at Meroë measures six square metres at its base. Amanitore is said to be mentioned in the Bible in the story about the conversion of the Ethiopian in Acts 8:26–40.

Amanitore is reputed to have been one of the great builders in Nubian history. After the destruction of the Temple of Amen in Napata during the Roman pushback, she embarked on a massive restoration effort. Amanitore also helped build Amen temples in Naqa and Amara and water reservoirs in Meroë.

Although it is uncertain whether Amanitore was the mother of Nakatamani, as queen mothers Kandakes were so powerful in the hierarchy of rulers in Nubia that they created their sons as rulers. They could also depose their own sons. In fact, a Kandake could order a king to commit suicide to end his rule. He was required to obey.

WHAT HAPPENED TO MEROË?

In 600 BC, following attacks by the Assyrians, the capital of Nubia was moved from Kerma to Napata and later to Meroë. The Assyrian Empire covered parts of modern-day Syria, Turkey, Iraq and Iran.

Meroë became very prosperous. Its wealth was partly based on trade and commerce, particularly after 2 BC when the camel was introduced and lucrative caravan routes developed across Africa. Meroë occupied a strategic position, with access to trading outlets on the Red Sea. Pottery, jewellery and woven cloth were all produced to a very high standard of craftsmanship.

The Nubian kingdom also had the resources that were needed to smelt iron ore: water from the Nile and wood from acacia trees to make charcoal. Iron gave the Meroites spears, arrows, and axes. Hoes allowed them to develop a mixed farming economy to exploit the full potential of the tropical summer rainfall.

Although Amen (Amun) was highly influential in the whole of Upper and Lower Egypt for more than a thousand years, Meroë developed its own forms of religious worship. The most important regional deity was the Lion God, Apedemek – often portrayed with a lion's head on a human body as with the sphinx.

The Kingdom of Meroë began to fade as a power by 2 AD with the decline of its traditional industries. The iron industry used huge quantities of charcoal, which led to deforestation and erosion of the land.

In around 350 AD, an army led by King Ezana, of the growing kingdom of neighbouring Axum in what is now Ethiopia, invaded Meroë. By then the Meroites had already dispersed, replaced by a people described by the Axumites as the Noba.

King Ezana converted to Christianity when the Roman Emperor Constantine called a bishops' conference at Nicea – modern-day Turkey – in 325 AD and adopted Christianity as the state religion. Ethiopia sent representatives. The Roman Empire became the third state to do so after Armenia and Georgia.

In 4 AD, Ethiopia became the fourth country to adopt Christianity. When Islam arose in 7 AD the Arabs invaded North Africa, between 639 and 642 AD and introduced Islam to the whole of North Africa and parts of the Sudan. Some descendants of the Noba, Nubians who had converted to Christianity, faced constant assaults from the Muslims for several years. Since then the whole of the region that was formerly the great civilization of Nubia or Kush has today been either Arabized or Christianized.

The state of Nubia had completely faded by 4 AD, followed by the collapse of the Roman Empire a century later in 476 AD, splitting into two.

Much about the Kingdom of Kush (Nubia) remains a mystery because no one has been able to translate the meroitic script. Most historical accounts were written by Greek and Roman historians and translated from Greek and Latin. Historians therefore do not know the Nubian side of the story. is quite possible that we have not yet heard the last word n the great Kandakes of Nubia.

MAKEDA QUEEN OF SHEBA

*Come into the garden of spice
Perfect Love has no price*

Many centuries ago, Makeda, Queen of Sheba ruled the Kingdom of Sheba, which today forms part of modern-day Ethiopia. She was one of the earliest known powerful Kandakes or Queens of the Nile Valley in Kush, also known as

Nubia, which covers parts of present-day Sudan and Ethiopia. Makeda's mother was called Queen Ismenie. Her father and grandfather were the last two rulers of the Za Besi Angabo Dynasty which lasted 350 years. The record of the rulers of the area previously called Shewa or Kush dates as far back as 5 000 years before Christ.

SO WHO WAS THE REAL QUEEN OF SHEBA?
Makeda became known when her story was told in the Christian Bible, the Muslim Koran , and in the holy book of Ethiopia called the Kebra Nagast (Glory of Kings). Much has also been written about her in various books, both fiction and non-fiction.

According to records in Ethiopia, Makeda was born in 1020 BC. Her father the king died 15 years later in 1005 BC and at the age of 15, Makeda became Queen and ruled Ethiopia for 40 years. At the time, Ethiopia had a very advanced civilization and was ruled by a line of virgin queens. In power and fame it was second in the world only to Kemet. Today we know Kemet as ancient Egypt because it was renamed Aigyptos by the Greeks who in 332 BC invaded the area and occupied it for the next 302 years.

Makeda was a very competent ruler; skilled in public relations and international diplomacy. She had a sweet voice and was said to be an excellent speaker. She was also very wise, intelligent, beautiful and hardworking.

However, what made her famous is the story of a royal visit

she paid to the biblical King Solomon who was, it is said, at the height of his glory after building a magnificent temple in Jerusalem. To announce this, Solomon sent invitations to various foreign countries for their merchants to come to Jerusalem to trade.

King Solomon was fascinated with Ethiopia's beautiful people, rich history, deep spiritual traditions and wealth. He sent for an important Ethiopian merchant by the name Tamrin who brought with him valuables like ebony, sapphires and red gold to sell to the King.

Tamrin was impressed by King Solomon and his young nation. He greatly admired the magnificent buildings, and was most amazed with Solomon's wisdom and compassion for his subjects. Tamrin returned to Ethiopia and reported his adventures to Queen Makeda. She was so fascinated with the exciting story that she decided to embark on a royal visit to Judah.

Before her trip, the Queen of Sheba told her subjects:

I love wisdom
Because it is far better
Than gold and silver
And sweeter than honey.

The Queen of Sheba then set out on her journey with many attendants in beautiful clothing. There were 800 camels, and donkeys and mules too numerous to count. In a blaze of glory

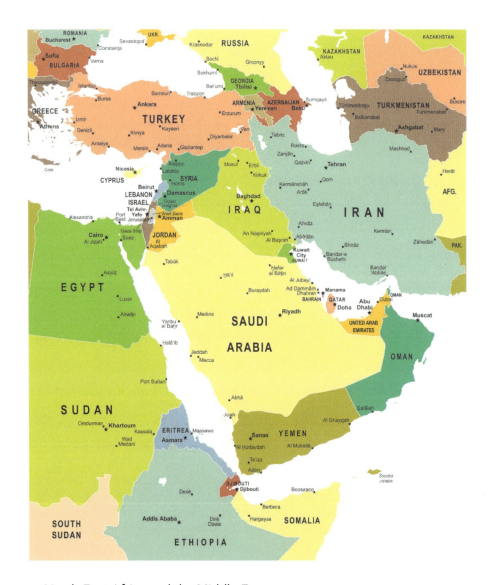

North-East Africa and the Middle East.

she travelled across the desert. Solomon was very surprised when he met this great, beautiful black queen. Besides being his equal in every respect, she was wise beyond her years. Makeda also brought with her many gifts – great quantities of gold, precious stones and spices. Solomon was dumbfounded and the whole of Judah marvelled.

Most of all, the Queen of Sheba loved wisdom. The real reason for her visit was to exchange wisdom with Solomon and test him with difficult questions. Solomon accepted the challenge and passed the exam with flying colours. He was in awe of the Queen of Sheba and went to great lengths to satisfy her every desire. A special apartment was built for her lodging and she was provided with the best food and many outfits.

In response to her request for knowledge he set up a throne for her beside his own. It was covered with silken carpets, adorned with fringes of gold and studded with diamonds and pearls. From her visitor's throne she listened while he delivered judgements. Queen Makeda also accompanied Solomon on a tour of his kingdom. She observed the spiritual leader as he interacted with his subjects in everyday affairs.

Solomon fell in love with the young virgin. He held banquets in her honour and entertained her throughout her royal visit.

According to Ethiopian tradition, the Queen was to remain chaste. Although Solomon knew this, he wanted an African son. During the six months of Makeda's visit, he tricked her into an affair.

Eventually Makeda had to go back to rule her Kingdom of Sheba. Solomon was heartbroken. When she and her entourage prepared to leave, he placed a ring on her finger and pleaded, "If you have a son, give this to him and send him back."

On her return to Sheba, Makeda did indeed have a son. She named him Bayna Lekhem, meaning "son of the wise man". He would be king after she died. When the young man became an adult, he wished to visit his father, so Makeda sent a message to Solomon to anoint their son as King of Ethiopia and to mandate that from then on only males descended from their son were to rule Sheba. Solomon and the Jewish people rejoiced when his son arrived in Israel. The King anointed him as requested and renamed him Menelik, which means "how handsome he is".

King Solomon, so the story goes, begged Menelik to remain in Israel but the young man refused. Solomon then called his leaders and nobles and announced that since he was sending his first-born son away, they should permit their sons to accompany him and serve as his counsellors and officers. They agreed to do so.

According to the Kebra Nagast, Menelik asked his father for a replica of the biblical Ark of the Covenant to accompany him to Sheba. It is written that while Solomon intended to grant his son's wish, the sons of the counsellors, angry at having to leave their homes, stole the real Ark and took it to

Sheba. Ethiopia still claims to have the real Ark.

It is said that Menelik, on returning to Sheba, ruled wisely and well. His famous lineage has been traced by the Ethiopians to the 20th century. Ethiopian rulers (Ras) call themselves the "conquering Lion of Judah" direct descendants of King Solomon and the Queen of Sheba.

According to the poets, Solomon, in trying to win the heart of Makeda, whispered to her:

> *When you are me*
> *And I am you*
> *Time is no more*
> *Forget that we are wise*
> *Gold and silver will pass away*
> *Come into the garden of spice*
> *Perfect love has no price.*

FURTHER READING

Adamu, M. (1984). *The Hausa and their neighbours in the central Sudan.* Niane, ed, 266-300.

Adeleye, R. A. (1971). *Hausaland and Borno 1600-1800. History of West Africa,* 1, 579-84.

Agbodeka, F. (1971). *African politics and British policy in the Gold Coast, 1868-1900: a study in the forms and force of protest.* [London]: Longman; [Evanston, Ill.]: Northwestern University Press.

Arnett, E. J. (1910). A Hausa chronicle. *Journal of the Royal African Society,* 9(34), 161-167.

Asante, M. K., & Mazama, A. (Eds.). (2005). *Encyclopedia of Black studies.* Sage.

Budge, E. A. W. (1906). *Cook's Handbook for Egypt and the Sûdân.* T. Cook & Son.

Butin, R. (1908). *Candace. In The Catholic Encyclopedia.* New York: Robert Appleton Company. Retrieved May 22, 2018 from New Advent: http://www.newadvent.org/cathen/03244c.htm

Carmichael, J. (2013). *African Eldorado: Gold Coast to Ghana.* Duckworth.

da Napoli, A. G. *La Maravigliosa Conversione alla Santa Fede di Cristo della Regina Singa e del svo Regno di Matamba nell'Africa Meridionale,* ed. Francesco Maria Gioia da Napoli (Naples, 1668).

Donkoh, Adu Boahene (2004). Yaa Asantewaa and the Asante-British War of 1900-1.

Fluehr-Lobban, C. (1998). *Nubian Queens in the Nile Valley and Afro-Asiatic Cultural History.* Boston: Museum of Fine Arts.

Foss, Michael (1999), *The Search for Cleopatra,* Arcade Publishing , ISBN 978-1-55970-503-5

Fraser, P. M. (1972). *Ptolemaic Alexandria (Vol. 2).* Clarendon Press.

Ginzberg, L., Szold, H., Bogdanovic, A., & Djordjevic, M. (1909). *The Legends of the Jews.*

Hegesippus Historiae i.29-32

Hubbard, D. A. (1956). The literary sources of the Kebra Nagast (Doctoral dissertation, University of St Andrews).

Jones, D. E. (1997). *Woman Warriors: A History.* Washington DC, London.

Jordan, H. (2018). *Njinga of Angola: Africa's Warrior Queen.* African Studies Quarterly, 17(4), 126-128.

Krige, E. J., & Krige, J. D. (1947). *The realm of a rain-queen: A study of the pattern of Lovedu society.* International institute of African languages & cultures.

Littmann, E. (Ed.). (1904). *The Legend of the Queen of Sheba in the Tradition of Axum (Vol. 1).* EJ Brill.

Mohale, M. R. (2014). Khelobedu cultural evolution through oral tradition (Doctoral dissertation).

Njoku, Onwuka N (1997). *Mbundu.* New York: The Rosen Publishing Group Inc. ISBN 0823920046.

Palmer, H. R. (1908). The Kano Chronicle. *The Journal of the Royal Anthropological Institute of Great Britain and Ireland*, 38, 58-98.

Pinches, T. G. (1923). *The Queen of Sheba and Her Only Son Menyelek.*

Plinius Secundus, C. (1906). *Naturalis historia.* vii.2.14, ix.58, 119-121, xxi.9.12

Walker, S., & Higgs, P. (Eds.). (2001). *Cleopatra of Egypt: from history to myth.* British Museum Press.

Weigall, A. E. P. B. (1914). *The Life and Times of Cleopatra, Queen of Egypt.* Putnam.

Wilks, I. (1989). *Asante in the Nineteenth Century: the structure and evolution of a political order.* CUP Archive.

Made in the USA
Middletown, DE
06 April 2020